THE WORLD'S MOST AMAZING
INVENTIONS FACTS
For Kids

Written and compiled by Guy Campbell & Mark Devins
Illustrated by Paul Moran

CONTENTS

Accidental Successes 6

If at First You Don't Succeed 16

Up, Up and Away 20

Watchamacallits 26

The Man with a Plan 28

What a Doll! 32

It's a Hit! 34

What's in a Name? 35

Just Do It! 36

Patently a Genius 38

Food, Glorious Food 40

What and When? 44

Wrong, Wrong, Wrong! 54

It'll Never Work 66

Wheel Smart 74

Spare Parts 76

From Foot to Ferrari 90

Celebrity Inventors 102

Mr Thunder & Lightning 108

ACCIDENTAL SUCCESSES

Inventions that Just Happened

The first match was accidentally invented in 1826 when chemist John Walker had been mixing a pot of potash and antimony with a stick in his workshop. He scraped the stick against the stone floor to remove the blob of dried mixture from the end of his stirrer, and it burst into flames.

In 1598, Dutch eyeglass maker Hans Lippershey was checking some new lenses by holding them up to the window. He discovered that if they were held the correct distance apart, one in front of the other, the image of the view outside became hugely magnified. He had just invented the telescope.

Innkeeper Ruth Wakefield was baking biscuits one day in the 1930s using a recipe that dated back a hundred years or so. She cut up a chocolate bar and put the chunks in the batter, expecting them to melt. She thought she'd be taking chocolate biscuits out of the oven. Instead, what she got were butter biscuits studded with chocolate pieces. Her mistake – chocolate chip cookies – became one of the world's most popular tea-time treats.

Will Keith Kellogg was the man behind the W.K. Kellogg Foundation, founded in 1906. In 1894, he was trying to improve the vegetarian diet of his hospital patients. While searching for a bread substitute, Kellogg accidentally left a pot of boiled wheat to stand on a hot stove. When Kellogg flattened the dried-out wheat with a roller, each grain emerged as a large, thin flake. The flakes turned out to be a tasty cereal. Kellogg had invented cornflakes!

In 1928, scientist Alexander Fleming found that one of the bacteria samples he had left by a window had gone mouldy. On closer examination he found that the mould was dissolving the harmful bacteria. That's how we got penicillin, one of the greatest medical discoveries in history, which helps people around the world recover from infections.

In the early 1940s, engineer James Wright was charged with a task of the utmost importance to the war effort: to develop a cheap substitute for rubber that could be used to produce tyres for military vehicles, gas masks and a whole host of military gear. Wright tackled the task diligently, working night and day to complete his task ... and ended up inventing Silly Putty. Over 200 million plastic eggs, containing 3,000 tons of Wright's Silly Putty, have been sold since 1949.

In 1928, 23-year-old Walter E. Diemer was working for the Fleer Chewing Gum Company in Philadelphia, USA. In his spare time he played around with new recipes. By accident, he made a batch that was less sticky than ordinary gum, and also stretched more easily. He discovered that with a little persuasion the gum could be used to blow bubbles! He took a lump of his new formula to a local shop, and it sold out in an afternoon. The people at Fleer marketed the creation and Diemer taught salesmen to blow bubbles, to demonstrate what made this gum different from other gums. They called it Dubble Bubble. Walter never got royalties from his invention, which would surely have made him a very wealthy man, but he didn't seem to mind. "I've done something with my life. I've made kids happy around the world," he said. "How many people can make that claim?"

While attempting to develop a super strong glue, 3M employee Spencer Silver accidentally developed a glue that was so weak it would barely hold two pieces of paper together. However, his colleague Art Fry had a use for it. Fry sang with his church choir and marked the pages of his hymnal with small scraps of paper that often fell out. He used Silver's glue to hold the papers in place. Today we call these Post-it™ Notes.

A workman who left the soap-mixing machine on too long was responsible for inventing Ivory Soap, one of the world's leading brands. He was so embarrassed by his mistake that he threw the mess in a stream. Imagine his dismay when the evidence of his error floated to the surface! Result: Ivory Soap, the soap that floats. The careless chap had whipped so much air into the mix that his batch of Ivory was lighter than water, making it much easier to find in the bath.

In the 1950s, George de Mestral came home from a walk in the woods to find his jacket covered with cockleburs – little plant pods with tiny spikes. Interested to see how they worked, De Mestral put the cockleburs under a microscope and saw that each spike ended in a little hook. George's curiosity lead him to the invention of Velcro.

Wilson Greatbatch, a medical researcher, was working on a device to record a patient's irregular heartbeat when he accidentally fitted a resistor of the wrong size into the device. The machine started to pulse, stopped, and pulsed again, just like a human heart. After two years of tinkering, Greatbatch had constructed the first implantable pacemaker. He later invented a corrosion-free lithium battery to power it, and millions have benefited since.

In 1942, Percy Le Baron Spencer was working with radar equipment when he noticed that a chocolate bar had melted in his pocket. Testing a theory, he held a bag of unpopped popcorn in front of the machine. It popped. It was a short step from this discovery to the invention of the microwave oven.

In 1982, researchers at a Japanese laboratory used Superglue to fix a crack in a fish tank. The fumes from the Superglue condensed on fingerprints that had been left on the tank, making them clearly visible. This discovery is now used by police forces the world over to catch criminals.

An extremely famous toy was the result of an attempt by engineer Richard James to produce an anti-vibration device for ship instruments. His goal was to develop a spring that would counterbalance the waves that rock a ship at sea. Instead, he invented the Slinky.

A baker named William Russell Frisbee, of Connecticut, USA, came up with a clever marketing idea back in the 1870s. He embossed the family name on the bottom of the tin plates in which his company's pies were sold. The pans were re-usable, so every time a customer baked a home-made pie, it would be stamped with the name Frisbee, reminding them of the pie that came with the tin. Frisbee's pies were sold throughout Connecticut, where, in the 1940s, students at the famous Yale University began flinging the pie tins through the air for sport. Ten years later, in California, Walter Morrison designed a disk for playing catch. It was made by the Wham-O toy company. On a promotional tour of colleges, the Wham-O president saw the pie-plate tossing craze at Yale. Morrison, no slouch at spotting a winning sales trick, called his flying saucer "Frisbee" after the pie plate from Connecticut.

IF AT FIRST YOU DON'T SUCCEED

Inventions that Took a While

A brilliantly successful but incredibly unlucky inventor, a blacksmith named Thomas Davenport, invented the first rotary electric motor. In 1836 he headed out on foot from his Vermont, USA, home to file a patent application at the Patent Office in Washington, D.C. By the time he got there, he had spent all his money and couldn't afford the $30 fee, so he had to turn around and walk all the way home. When he later posted his application with money he'd raised, the Patent Office was destroyed in a fire. He did finally get credit for his invention on February 5, 1837.

Kleenex tissue was originally designed to be a gas mask filter. It was developed at the beginning of World War One to replace cotton, which was then in high demand by army medics as a surgical dressing.

Canadian inventors Chris Haney, Scott Abbott and John Haney struggled for four years to get anyone interested in their new invention – a quiz-based board game. While it took them only 45 minutes to come up with the idea for the game, they lost $45,000 trying to market it before it finally became a hit. The game was called Trivial Pursuit, and eventually it became a massive worldwide success, but not before it took its creators to the brink of bankruptcy. Unemployed artist Michael Wurstlin designed the board and logo for Trivial Pursuit in exchange for five shares in the company. Despite the early failure, by 1986 his shares were valued at two and a half million dollars.

Frank Epperson, then eleven years old, invented the ice lolly by accident. One day little Frank mixed some soda water powder and water, which was a popular drink in those days. He left the mixture on the back porch overnight with the stirring stick still in it. The temperature dropped to a record low that night and the next day Frank took the stick of frozen soda water to show his friends at school. Eighteen years later, in 1923, Frank remembered his frozen soda water mixture and began a business producing "Epsicles" in seven fruity versions. The name was later changed to the "Popsicle". Over three million Popsicle ice lollies are now sold each year.

UP, UP AND AWAY

The Inventions of Flight

1783

First balloon flight. Jacques and Joseph Montgolfier of Annonay, France, sent up a small, smoke-filled balloon.

1784

First powered balloon. General Jean Baptiste Marie Meusnier developed the first propeller-driven balloon – the crew cranking three propellers to give the craft a speed of about five km/h (three mph).

1797

First parachute jump. André-Jacques Garnerin dropped from about 2,000 metres (6,500 feet) over Monceau Park in Paris.

1852

First dirigible (balloon or airship that can be directed). Henri Giffard, a French engineer, flew in a controllable steam-engine-powered balloon from Paris to Trappe.

1900

First zeppelin flight. Germany's Count Ferdinand von Zeppelin flew the first of his long series of rigid-frame airships. It attained a speed of 29 km/h (18 mph).

1903

First successful heavier-than-air machine flight. Aviation was really born at Kitty Hawk when Orville Wright took to the air. He covered 120 feet in twelve seconds. Later that day, in one of four flights, Wilbur stayed up 59 seconds and covered 260 metres (852 feet).

1913

First multi-engined aircraft. Built and flown by a Russian, Igor Ivan Sikorsky.

1914

First aerial combat. In August, Allied and German pilots started shooting at each other with pistols and rifles, unsuccessfully.

1918

First airmail service. Operated for the Post Office by the US Army, the first service started with one round trip a day between Washington, D.C. and New York City.

1929

First rocket-engine flight. Fritz von Opel, a German car maker, stayed aloft in his small rocket-powered craft for 75 seconds.

1931

First flight into the stratosphere. Auguste Piccard, a Swiss physicist, and Charles Knipfer ascended in a balloon from Augsburg, Germany, and reached a height of 15,787 metres (51,793 feet) in a 17-hour flight.

1937

First successful helicopter flight. Hanna Reitsch, a German pilot, flew a Focke FW-61 at Bremen. Ms Reitsch was also the first female civil and military aviation test pilot.

1942

First American jet plane flight. Robert Stanley, chief pilot for Bell Aircraft, flew the Bell XP-59 Airacomet at Muroc Army Base, California, USA.

1944

First production stage rocket-engine fighter plane. The German Messerschmitt Me 163B Komet became operational in June 1944.

1947

First piloted supersonic flight in an aeroplane. Captain Charles E. Yeager, US Air Force, flew the X-1 rocket-powered research plane faster than the speed of sound at Muroc Air Force Base, California, USA.

1952

First jetliner service. The BOAC De Havilland Comet flight started between London and Johannesburg, South Africa.

1958

First transatlantic jet passenger services. BOAC, New York to London, and Pan American, New York to Paris.

1968

Prototype of world's first supersonic airliner. The Soviet-designed Tupolev Tu-144 made its first flight on December 31.

1976

First regularly scheduled commercial supersonic transport flights begin. Air France and British Airways inaugurated Concorde service. Air France flew the Paris–Rio de Janeiro route, and British Airways flew from London to Bahrain.

1977

First successful human-powered aircraft. Paul MacCready was awarded the Kremer Prize for creating the Gossamer Condor, which was flown by Bryan Allen over a five-kilometre (three-mile) course. The super-light craft was pedal-propelled.

1979

First long-distance solar-powered flight. Janice Brown, a former teacher, flew Solar Challenger for ten kilometres (six miles) in Arizona. The craft's engine was powered by the sun.

2001

First solar-powered flight to the edge of space. NASA's solar-powered plane Helios reached an altitude of 30,000 metres (96,500 feet) during a flight over Hawaii, breaking not only the 24,445-metre (80,200-feet) record for propeller-driven aircraft, but the 25,929-metre (85,068-feet) record for all non-rocket aircraft.

WATCHAMACALLITS

How Inventions Got Their Names

"Patent leather" got its name because the process of applying the polished black finish to leather was once patented.

The snorkel was named after the German word for periscope.

Possibly America's most famous sportsman ever was New York Yankees baseball legend Babe Ruth, and one of America's most celebrated chocolate bars is called "Baby Ruth". There is no connection between the two. The bar was named after President Grover Cleveland's daughter, Ruth, and not the baseball player.

A car's instrument panel is called a dashboard. The term dates back to horse and cart days when dashing horses kicked up mud, splashing the passengers riding behind them. The dashboard was invented to protect them.

THE MAN WITH A PLAN

Leonardo da Vinci

Born in 1452, there appears to be no field of knowledge to which Leonardo da Vinci has not made a contribution.

Anatomy, physics, mechanics, writing, engineering, mathematics, philosophy and botany were all advanced by his genius. Leonardo made the first studies of flight in the 1480s. His Ornithopter flying machine was never created, but the modern-day helicopter is based on the concept. He applied his drawing skills to architecture, canal building and weapons design, and worked for the Duke of Milan as a military engineer, inventing weapons and fortifications.

As military engineer and architect to the Pope's son, Cesare Borgia, Leonardo proposed creating a massive wooden bridge across the eight-kilometre- (five-mile-) wide Gulf of Istanbul. The plan seems like fantasy, but modern engineers have determined that it would have been completely sound.

He drew up plans for a bicycle, a helicopter, an "auto-mobile", a steam-powered cannon, waterwheels, and many industrial machines powered by flowing water.

He also devised plans to cover Milan with canals, and sketched a submarine and an unsinkable double-hulled ship, as well as dredgers for clearing harbours and channels.

He became a civil engineer and architect, building bridges and aqueducts, and as a military engineer he was centuries ahead of his time, designing rudimentary tanks, catapults, machine guns and naval weaponry. His creative and visionary inventiveness has yet to be matched.

Some of da Vinci's side projects included: parachutes, underwater breathing devices, ocean rescue equipment, lathes, pumps, water turbines, swing bridges, cranes, street lights, mechanical saws, contact lenses and scissors.

And in his spare time away from inventing, he proposed – unbelievably to most people at the time – that the Earth rotates around the Sun, and he created the first ever textbook of human anatomy, drawn from the real corpses of executed criminals which he cut up and sketched. Oh, and he was one of the greatest painters of his time, creating (among other celebrated works) the *Mona Lisa* – the single most famous painting in history.

WHAT A DOLL!

The Barbie Story

The Barbie Doll was based on a real human being. She was Barbara Handler, the daughter of Ruth and Elliot Handler.

In the early 1950s, Ruth saw that her daughter and her friends liked playing with adult dolls more than baby dolls. Because all the adult dolls then available were made of paper or cardboard, Barbara decided to create a three-dimensional adult female doll. She took her idea to the advertising executives at Mattel Corp., the company that she and her husband, Elliot, had started some years before. The executives rejected the idea as too expensive and with no potential for wide market appeal. Soon after, Barbara returned from Europe with a "Lilli" doll, modelled after a character in a German comic strip. She designed a doll similar to Lilli, hiring a designer to make clothes, and the result was the Barbie. Mattel finally agreed to back it, and Barbie was launched at the New York Toy Fair in 1959.

Barbie set a new sales record for Mattel in her first year on the market: 351,000 dolls, at three dollars each. Today, with over one billion dolls sold, the Barbie product line is the most successful in the history of toys.

Barbie has been joined by friends and family over the years, including Ken (named after the Handlers' son) in 1961, Midge in 1963, Skipper in 1965 and Christie (an African-American doll) in 1968. In 1995, Barbie got a little sister, Baby Sister Kelly (known as Shelly in the UK), and, in 1997, a friend in a wheelchair, Share-a-Smile Becky.

IT'S A HIT!

Toy Hits Through the Century

1900	**1974**
Baseball cards	Lego
1901	**1975**
Ping-pong	Skateboard
1902	**1977**
Teddy bear	Slime
1909	**1980**
Jigsaw puzzle	Rubik's Cube
1929	**1983**
Yo-yo	Cabbage Patch dolls
1933	**1989**
Monopoly	Nintendo
1943	**1990**
Scrabble	Rollerblades
1957	**1994**
Frisbee	Beanie Babies
1959	**1996**
Barbie doll	Buzz Lightyear
1960	**1998**
Toy Trolls	Furby
1971	**2002**
Space Hopper	Playstation 2

WHAT'S IN A NAME?

Brand Names that Are the Product

Chapstick	–	Lip balm
Hoover	–	Vacuum cleaner
Kleenex	–	Facial tissues
Rollerblades	–	In-line skates
Sellotape	–	Sticky tape
Styrofoam	–	Plastic foam
Teflon	–	Nonstick coating
Vaseline	–	Petroleum jelly
Velcro	–	Hook and loop fastener
Walkman	–	Portable cassette
Xerox	–	Photocopier

JUST DO IT!

Inventing in Ten Steps

1 Make sketches of your invention.
2 Visit shops. Check out the competition.
3 Find out all about your future customers.
4 Patent your invention. This can cost upwards of £600 and take up to two years. Get an agent if you can afford it.
5 Build and test a small-scale prototype of your invention that demonstrates its uses.
6 Make a plan of how you will make money with your invention.
7 Sell your invention to others or start your own business selling it yourself.
8 Find manufacturers, arrange meetings.
9 Participate at trade shows.
10 Licence your invention to manufacturers and hope your product is a hit!

PATENTLY A GENIUS

Thomas Alva Edison

Thomas Alva Edison (1847–1931) was an American inventor and businessman. He is best known for his invention of the electric light, the phonograph (record player), and movies.

He also started his own newspaper, the *Weekly Herald*, the first paper to be printed and sold on a train. His profits went into setting up his own chemistry lab. When his mother complained of the smell, he moved his lab onto the train as well. Unfortunately, the moving train caused some phosphorous to spill, setting fire to some luggage, and he was asked to leave. So by 1869 he was a full-time inventor. His first idea to receive a patent was the electric vote recorder.

In 1876 he opened a lab in New Jersey. He planned to build a small invention every ten days, and a large invention every six months.

Here he invented the phonograph and the electric light system, and tried to invent the telephone, but Alexander Graham Bell beat him to it. In 1878 he set up the Edison Electric Light Company, and in 1887, he built a new lab in West Orange, New Jersey, where he invented the motion picture camera, the alkaline storage battery, the electric pen (an early printer), and improved the phonograph so that it could be sold commercially.

After his death on October 17, 1931, lights were dimmed for one minute throughout the United States, as a sign of respect and mourning. During his life Edison amassed an incredible 2,332 US and foreign patents.

FOOD, GLORIOUS FOOD

Edible Inventions

New inventions are often called "the best thing since sliced bread", making them the best thing since 1912, when Otto Frederick Rohwedder invented the bread slicer. First he came up with a device that held slices together with hat pins, which was a disaster. In 1928, he designed a machine that both sliced and wrapped.

The original name for French fries was "potatoes, fried in the French manner" – that is how US President Thomas Jefferson first described the dish. Jefferson introduced French fries to the Americans in the late 1700s on his return from diplomatic duties in Europe.

John Montague, Fourth Earl of Sandwich, born in 1718, was the originator of the sandwich. Montague loved to eat beef between slices of toast. He also loved to gamble. The sandwich allowed the Earl to have one hand free for card playing, without having to stop for supper.

The origin of the hamburger is unknown, but the hamburger patty and sandwich were probably brought by 19th-century German immigrants to the United States, where, in a matter of decades, it came to be considered the all-American food. The trademark for the name "cheeseburger" was awarded in 1935 to Louis Ballast of the Humpty Dumpty Drive-In, in Denver, Colorado.

One day in 1853, at Moon Lake Lodge in Saratoga Springs, USA, Cornelius Vanderbilt refused to eat an order of French fries because they were too thick. The chef, George Crum, decided this complaint was unreasonable. To teach the picky diner a lesson, he sliced a potato paper-thin and fried it so heavily it could not be cut with a fork. But Mr Vanderbilt loved them, and potato chips (or crisps) were born.

Caleb Bradham of North Carolina, USA, was a pharmacist. Like many pharmacists at the turn of the century, he had a soda fountain in his shop, where he served his customers refreshing drinks that he created himself. His most popular beverage was created in the summer of 1898. 'Brad's Drink' was made of carbonated water, sugar, vanilla, rare oils, pepsin and cola nuts. The drink was later renamed Pepsi-Cola after the pepsin and cola nuts used in the recipe. In 1940, the first ever nationally broadcast advertising jingle was for Pepsi. The jingle was called "Nickel Nickel" and referred to the price of a can. It became a huge hit record worldwide and was recorded in 55 languages.

The word "ketchup" comes from the Chinese "ke-tsiap", a pickled fish sauce. It made its way to Malaysia where it became "kechap". Heinz began selling tomato ketchup in 1876.

WHAT AND WHEN?

A Brief History of Food Inventions

1872 Blackjack chewing gum
1886 Coca-Cola
1897 Campbell's condensed soup
1898 Shredded Wheat breakfast cereal
1902 Pepsi-Cola
1904 Dr Pepper
1904 Peanut butter
1904 Popcorn
1906 Kellogg's Corn Flakes
1910 Tea bags
1912 Hellmann's mayonnaise
1921 Wrigley's gum
1928 Rice Krispies
1929 Lithiated Lemon (later 7-Up)
1930 Snickers chocolate bar

1936 Mars Bar

1937 Kit Kat chocolate bar

1937 Smarties

1937 Spam

1938 Nescafé (first instant coffee)

1940 McDonald's

1941 Cheerioats (renamed Cheerios in 1946)

1941 M&Ms

1950 Dunkin' Donuts

1954 Burger King

1955 Kentucky Fried Chicken

1958 Pizza Hut

1959 Häagen-Dazs ice cream

1968 McDonald's Big Mac

1969 Sugar-free gum

1971 Starbucks

1977 McDonald's Happy Meals

1982 Diet Coke

1984 Ben & Jerry's ice cream

Around 1500 BC, the Olmec Indians of the Gulf of Mexico were the first to grow cocoa beans as a domestic crop. 2,000 years later, chocolate as a drink became popular among the rich Aztec upper classes, who called it *xocalatl*, meaning "warm or bitter liquid". In 1502, Christopher Columbus encountered a Mayan trading canoe in Guanaja carrying cocoa beans as cargo. Soon afterwards, the drink became popular in Spain, and the Spanish added sugar and vanilla to sweeten the brew. A hundred years later, chocolate rolls and cakes were served in chocolate emporiums all over Europe. In 1795, Dr Joseph Fry of Bristol, England, employed a steam engine for grinding cocoa beans, an invention that led to the manufacture of chocolate on a large scale and, in 1847, Joseph Fry & Son discovered a way to mix the cocoa butter so that it could be moulded. The result was the first modern chocolate bar.

Some names of chocolate bars that were introduced in the 1920s include: Milk Nut Loaf, Fat Emmas, Big Dearos, Vegetable Sandwich, Kandy Kake, Oh Henry! and the Chicken Dinner, a chocolate peanut roll that actually survived until the 1960s.

The Three Musketeers bar was introduced in 1932 and has lasted ever since as one of America's most popular snacks. Today, it's a single bar, but the original Three Musketeers had 3 bars in one wrapper, each made to a different recipe.

Seven billion pounds of chocolate and sweets are manufactured each year in the United States.

Cheesecake is believed to have been invented in ancient Greece. It was served to the athletes during the first Olympic Games held in 776 BC.

The origins of ice cream can be traced back to the 4th century BC, when the Roman Emperor Nero sent servants up nearby mountains to collect ice, which was combined with fresh fruit and honey to make a cooling dessert. In 6th-century China, cooks found a method of creating ice and milk mixtures, and ice cream was probably brought back from China by traders and introduced to Europe.

The first ice-cream parlour in America opened in New York City in 1776, and the treat became available to a much wider audience with the invention of refrigeration.

The "ice-cream sundae" was first created in 1881 by ice-cream shop-owner Ed Berners of Wisconsin, USA. Berners served his creation only on Sundays.

In 1904, Charles E. Menches of St Louis, USA, filled pastry cups with scoops of ice cream, thereby inventing the ice-cream cone. The take-away cone made its debut later that year at the St Louis World's Fair.

Over the centuries, the pizza was developed among the people of Naples, Italy. The modern pizza, with mozzarella cheese and tomato, was first made there by baker Raffaele Esposito in 1889, especially for the visit of Italian King Umberto I and Queen Margherita. This patriotic pizza of basil, tomato and mozzarella matched the new Italian flag's red, green and white, and became the Margherita, named after Her Majesty.

The little circular thing that keeps the pizza from hitting the inside of the box top is called a "package saver for pizza and cakes". It was invented by Carmela Vitale of New York, who filed for a US patent on February 10, 1983.

Clarence Birdseye invented a method for quick-freezing food in 1923. He sold the patents in 1929 for 22 million dollars.

The ancient Romans made toast. Tostum is the Latin word for scorching or burning.

The first electric toaster was invented in 1893 in the UK by Crompton and Co. It toasted one side of the bread at a time and it required a person to stand by and turn it off manually when the toast looked done. Charles Strite invented the modern pop-up toaster with a timer in 1919.

Thomas Adams tried to make chicle – a rubbery substance found in some trees – into car tyres and rain boots, without much success. One day, he absent-mindedly popped a piece of chicle into his mouth. Chewing away, he had the idea to add flavouring to the stuff. Shortly after, he opened the world's first chewing gum factory. In February 1871, Adams' New York Gum went on sale in shops for a penny a piece, and in 1888, an Adams' chewing gum called Tutti-Frutti became the first chewing gum to be sold in a vending machine.

In 1756, mayonnaise was invented in France by the chef of Duke de Richelieu. In 1905, the first ready-made mayonnaise was sold at Richard Hellman's New York delicatessen. In 1912, Richard's mayonnaise was mass marketed and sold under the name "Hellman's Blue Ribbon Mayonnaise".

Powdered milk was invented by ancient Mongolians, possibly as long as a thousand years ago. Italian traveller Marco Polo arrived in Mongolia in 1275 and stayed in Kublai Khan's court. Polo made written records of how the Mongols used powdered milk. They added millet and rice to milk, boiled it until thick, then let it dry.

A "Spork" is a cross between a spoon and a fork, sometimes called the "runcible spoon". A patent for the Spork was issued on August 11, 1970 to Van Brode Milling Company, of Massachusetts, USA.

WRONG, WRONG, WRONG!

Who Said Inventing was Easy?

Walter Hunt had no trouble thinking up new ideas. He invented a machine to spin cloth, a fire-engine gong, a forest saw, and a stove that burned hard coal. His inventions worked, but he never made any money from them. In 1849 he needed to pay a 15-dollar debt to a friend, so he came up with a new invention. From a piece of brass wire, coiled at the centre and shielded at one end, he made the first safety pin. He took out a patent on it, sold the rights for $400, paid his friend back and had $385 to spare. Then he watched his latest brainstorm go on to become a million- dollar money earner for someone else.

18th-century engineer Robert Fulton had to work hard to attract investors to build his new steamboat. The investors had one request; they asked that their names be kept secret in case people laughed at them for investing in a project that sounded so ridiculous.

Stock salesman Joshua Coppersmith was trying to sell stocks in a new telephone company in Boston, USA. He was arrested as a con-man for selling stocks in something that couldn't be done. People at the time thought it was impossible to send a voice over a wire.

In 1894, the President of the Royal Society in Britain, Lord Kelvin, predicted that radio had no future. The first radio factory opened five years later, and now there are over one billion radio sets in the world and more than 33,000 radio stations. He also predicted that heavier-than-air flying machines were impossible.

Mike Nesmith is a former member of the 1960s pop band the Monkees. His mother, Bette Nesmith Graham, was a creative individual herself. Her invention, liquid paper, was initially rejected by corporate giants IBM, so she set up her own cottage industry to make and sell it herself. She later sold the business for 47.5 million dollars.

With the advent of railways in the 19th century, one prominent American citizen proclaimed that they would create the need for dozens of new insane asylums to house all those who were driven mad by the noise and terrified by the size of the trains. The reputation of these new-fangled trains was no better in Europe. German experts predicted that if passenger trains travelled faster than 24 km/h (15 mph), the passengers would all get nosebleeds.

When Harry M. Warner, head of the Hollywood film studio Warner Brothers, was told about the possibility of movies with sound, he said, "Who the hell wants to hear actors talk?"

A Yale University management professor told one of his students, Fred Smith, that although his project idea was interesting, to earn better than a "C" grade, the idea had to be possible as well. Fred Smith's paper was a business proposal for a company offering a reliable overnight delivery service. He went on to found Federal Express.

When G. G. Hubbard learned of his future son-in-law's invention, he called it "only a toy". His daughter was engaged to a young man named Alexander Graham Bell, and the toy was the telephone.

"But what ... is it good for?" asked an engineer at the Advanced Computing Systems Division of IBM, in 1968, commenting on the microchip.

Even the inventor of the telephone, Alexander Graham Bell, didn't fully appreciate its future worldwide popularity, stating that it would be "useful for lonely farmers' wives".

"The wireless music box has no imaginable commercial value. Who would pay for a message sent to nobody in particular?" commented David Sarnoff's associates in response to his urgings for investment in radio in the 1920s.

Radio inventor Guiglelmo Marconi felt it might be a "useful replacement for Morse code wires".

Thomas Edison invented lots of things but he didn't invent the radio. In 1922 he declared that "the radio craze will die out in time."

When British merchant Peter Durand invented the metal can in 1810, he completely overlooked the need for a device to open it. The tin opener was invented some decades later.

When IBM conducted a market study of Chester Carlson's invention in 1959, the company concluded that it would take only 5,000 units of his new product to saturate the market. IBM therefore declined to be part of the new product introduction. Too bad for IBM. Carlson's invention was the photocopier, and his new product was the beginning of the Xerox Corporation. It is estimated that every day, worldwide, 3,000,000,000 photocopies are made.

In the early 20th century, a world market for only four million automobiles was forecast because it was thought the world would run out of chauffeurs.

Darryl F. Zanuck, of movie studios 20th Century Fox, thought television was just a passing fancy. In 1946, he said, "Television won't be able to hold any market after the first six months. People will soon get tired of staring at a plywood box every night."

Farmers rejected the first successful cast-iron plough in 1797. They believed the cast iron would poison the land and stimulate weeds, and in the mid-1800s, farmers tore down miles of new telegraph wire, fearful that the new fangled invention would disturb the weather and ruin crops.

Shortly after the end of World War Two in 1945, the whole of Volkswagen – the factory and all the patents – was offered, free, to Henry Ford, boss of the Ford Motor Company. He turned it down, dismissing the Volkswagen Beetle as a bad design. The Beetle became the best-selling vehicle of all time.

The telephone was not widely appreciated for the first 15 years of its existence because people did not see a use for it. In fact, in the British Parliament it was mentioned there was no need for telephones because "we have enough messengers here". Western Union, a US telegraph company, believed that it could never replace the telegraph. In 1876, an internal memo read: "This telephone has too many shortcomings to be seriously considered as a means of communication." Famous author, Mark Twain, upon being invited by Alexander Graham Bell to invest $5,000 in the new invention, could not see a future in the telephone, and turned him down.

"Computers in the future may weigh no more than 15 tons." – *Popular Mechanics* **magazine forecasting the relentless march of science in 1949.**

While still at college, Steve Jobs and Steve Wozniak took an invention they had been working on to Hewlett-Packard. They were told to come back when they'd left school. They didn't bother. The invention Hewlett-Packard turned down was the world's first personal computer. The two Steves went on to start their own company, Apple Computer Inc. The first Apple computer was born in Steve Jobs' parents' garage. Jobs and Wozniak worked furiously in that garage assembling computers for fellow students and were totally unprepared for their first commercial order for 50 computers. To raise the $1,300 needed for parts, Jobs sold his old Volkswagen camper van and Wozniak sold his Hewlett-Packard calculator. The next year, 1977, Apple sales reached $800,000. It was included on the Fortune 500 (a list of the largest US companies) in a record five years.

An eminent Irish scientist, Dr Dionysius Lardner (1793–1859) didn't believe that trains could contribute much in speedy transport. He wrote: "Travel at high speed is not possible, because passengers "would die of asphyxia [suffocation]". Today, trains reach speeds of 500 km/h (310 mph).

American physicist Robert Goddard's theory that rockets could operate in outer space met with a lot of criticism. Indeed, the New York Times printed an article ridiculing his ideas. The day after Apollo 11 left earth's orbit for the moon, largely due to Goddard's work, the newspaper published an apology.

But perhaps the guy who got it wrong most was the director of the United States Patent Office in 1899. He assured President William McKinley that "everything that can be invented has already been invented".

IT'LL NEVER WORK

Really Strange Inventions

12 Gauge Golf Club
US Patent 4,176,537

This golf club features a barrel, muzzle and a trap door in the back for loading an explosive charge. The firing pin is aligned so that when your club strikes the ball, it is literally blasted down the course!

Flying Fish
US patent 3,598,121

This angler's aid takes the sweat out of catching a big fish. A balloon floats on the water above your baited hook. When you feel a pull on your line, press the button on your fishing rod. The balloon fills with gas and your fish floats up out of the water!

Gravestone Sundial
French Patent 2780195

In this invention, a spike casts a shadow on the gravestone. At certain times of the year, the shadow points to the deceased's dates of birth, death and life events carved onto the gravestone, keeping passers-by informed of all the anniversaries of the person's life, even after their passing.

Junior Jail
US Patent 4,205,966

Changing a baby can be difficult when the baby doesn't want to be changed. But Junior Jail's "torso clamp" and foot and arm restraints mean that a baby can be practically bolted to a table while its nappy is changed.

Imaginary Pet Leash
International Patent WO9701384

This leash holds its shape as you walk and incorporates the lead and the collar in one. A tiny speaker in the collar is connected to switches in the leash handle, enabling the user to produce barks, growls and other appropriate pet noises on demand.

Snow Irrigator
UK Patent 1047735

This device pipes snow and ice balls from Antarctica to water the Australian desert, thereby solving the world food problem. The snowballs accelerate under gravity from 3,000 metres (10,000 feet) up on the Antarctic plateau, reaching speeds of up to 500 miles per hour, when they are shot through the pipelines thousands of miles long, using Earth's gravity and spinning energy to help them on their way,

Phone Gas
US Patent 5,308,063

This is an ingenious device for the parents of sick children who refuse to take their medicine. The medicine is contained in an inhaler in your telephone receiver. You call your child to the phone, which plays soothing music. Then at the push of a magic button, you gas him or her with the medicine, which comes squirting out of the mouthpiece!

Skin Stencil
US Patent 5,256,595

This is a cap designed with the sports fan in mind. It allows the cap wearer to actually burn his team's logo onto his forehead! The Skin Stencil has a cut-out design in the headband of the cap. The area around the cutout stencil blocks the sun from tanning your skin, while the logo will bronze onto your head!

Golf Practice Device
UK Patent 1251780

Light sensitive cells monitor the path of the club head as you swing it. If they detect that the player is about play a bad shot, and risk losing the ball in tall grass somewhere, a puff of compressed air passes along a pipe by the ball up into the middle of the tee. This blows the ball off the tee so that the player misses it completely, saving hours of ball-searching time.

Floating Furniture
US patent 4,888,836

This is a solution for people who live in small houses and have tables and chairs that are taking up too much space. This lighter-than-air inflatable furniture can be blown up with helium gas and stored on your ceiling when you're not using it! Need a nap? Just grab the tether rope and pull your bed off the ceiling! Also you can let the dining table float up to the ceiling after dinner, taking the dirty dishes out of your sight!

Dog Watch
US patent 5,023,850

A dog year is equal to seven human years, yes? Well then, every dog needs a watch that goes seven times faster than a normal one so he can tell the time too! The Dog Watch means Fido always knows how old he is, and he'll never be late for dinner!

Crunch Protector
US Patent 4,986,334

Everyone hates it when their breakfast cereal goes soggy. Well, you need suffer no longer with Crunch Protector! Simply fill the container under the milk bowl with sand to counter the weight of the cereal in the upper bowl. Now pour the cornflakes down the chute to the awaiting milk in the lower bowl and eat. Continue pouring and eating and pouring and eating. Each bite remains crunchy to the bottom of the bowl, ensuring breakfast satisfaction every time!

WHEEL SMART

Street Transport Takes Off

In-line skates were created back in the early 1700s when a Dutchman attached wooden spools to strips of wood and nailed them to his shoes. In 1980, two brothers from Minnesota, USA, Scott and Brennan Olsen, discovered an old in-line skate in a sports shop and thought the design would be perfect for off-season hockey training. They improved it and soon were manufacturing the first "Rollerblades" in their parents' basement. Hockey players and skiers soon caught on. Today 60 in-line skate manufacturers exist, but Rollerblades were the first with heel brakes and Active Brake Technology, and have over 200 other registered patents.

The skateboard started as a way of surfing on land. In the 1950s, Californian surfers, frustrated with bad weather, nailed the bases of roller skates to wooden planks. These boards allowed for "sidewalk surfing" down hills. The fad spread, and challenges were added, such as kerb-jumping. This became "street surfing". By the early 1970s, bike and toy companies were making boards with urethane wheels on flexible mounts. Riders' abilities improved along with the equipment. Skateboarding developed new moves, like the "Ollie", invented by Alan Ollie Gelf: it's a leap into the air during which the board stays flush with the feet. The empty swimming pools and building sites used for boarding were replaced by specially designed parks.

In 2003, skateboarding was America's sixth largest participant sport and, not content with the streets, the surfers are taking over the snow too!

SPARE PARTS

Invention Bits & Pieces

The inventor of the World Wide Web, British-born Tim Berners-Lee, never made any money from his invention, which completely changed the computer world. In 1989 he came up with a way to link documents on the Internet using hypertext, so "surfers" could jump from one document to another through highlighted words. He decided not to patent his technology since he feared that, if he did patent it, use of the Web would be too expensive and would therefore not become used worldwide. He passed up a certain fortune so that the world could learn and communicate.

Coca-Cola was originally green.

In the early 1970s, Hungarian architect Erno Rubik designed geometric models in his spare time and came up with a cube, with each face consisting of nine smaller cubes. He used it to teach algebraic group theory, but a Hungarian trading company saw its potential as a toy and began marketing it. By 1980, more than 100 million Rubik's Cubes had been sold around the world, as well as another 50 million "knock-off" cubes produced illegally by rival toymakers. More than 50 books were published explaining how to solve the puzzle.

The computer was launched in 1943, more than 100 years after Charles Babbage designed the first one. Babbage dropped his idea after he couldn't raise money for it. In 1998, the Science Museum in London built a working replica of Babbage's machine, using the materials available at Babbage's time. It worked just as Babbage had intended.

The yo-yo may be the second oldest toy in the world after the doll. There are ancient Greek yo-yos in museums in Athens and yo-yos are pictured on the walls of Egyptian temples.

Carving and playing with yoyos is a traditional pastime in the Philippines, but when Phillipino Pedro Flores moved to the USA in the 1920s and worked as a bellhop at a Santa Monica hotel, he found his lunchtime hobby was drawing a crowd! He started a company to make the toys, and sold it, together with the name "Yoyo" in 1929 to Donald F. Duncan. Duncan introduced the looped slip-string (which allows for advanced tricks), the first plastic yo-yos and the Butterfly-shaped yo-yo. Donald Duncan made a fortune, but lost it all again when the 1950s fad ended, largely through fighting costly court cases trying to stop competitors from making their own versions.

In 1879, Auguste Bartholdi received a design patent for the Statue of Liberty.

Eight-year-old Theresa Thompson and her nine-year-old sister, Mary, received a US patent in 1960. They had invented a solar-heated tent, which they called a "Wigwarm".

Six-year-old Suzanna Goodin, tired of cleaning the cat food spoon, invented an edible spoon-shaped cracker for pets. She won a grand prize for her idea in a National Invention Contest.

Melting ice cream inspired the invention of the outboard motor. Ole Evinrude was rowing his boat to his local island picnic spot and, as he rowed, his ice cream melted in the sun. Ole started thinking about making the trip quicker so he could enjoy his picnic unmelted. He invented the outboard motor, a handy device for any boater worried about their dessert.

The formulas for Cola-Cola and Silly Putty have never been patented. These trade secrets are shared with only a few company employees. There have been many attempts to duplicate the products, but so far, none has been successful.

Bar codes were invented by Bernard Silver and Norman Woodland in 1948, but it was over twenty years before the first bar-coded item was sold. It was a pack of Wrigley's chewing gum in 1974.

More than a million people got Pet Rocks for Christmas in 1975. Gary Dahl, of Los Gatos, California, was joking with friends about his easy-to-care-for pet, a rock! It ate nothing and didn't bark or chew the furniture. The Pet Rock was sold with a funny manual that included tips on how to teach it tricks. By 1976, Gary was a millionaire many times over.

Arthur Melin and Richard Knerr, founders of the Wham-O toy company, took an idea from Australia, where students exercised using bamboo hoops, and turned it into the biggest fad of all time. The Hula Hoop is a round plastic tube that can be rotated around the waist by swinging the hips. It can also be jumped through, skipped over, or spun around the neck. Four months after the launch, Wham-O had sold over twenty million of them.

A huge fad in the mid 1970s, Mood Rings were made of heat-sensitive liquid crystals encased in quartz. When the body temperature of the wearer changed, the crystals changed colour, supposedly indicating the wearer's mood. Blue meant happy; red meant insecure; green meant active; black meant tense. Joshua Reynolds, a 33-year-old New Yorker, was the creative genius behind them.

Long before starring in *Toy Story*, Mr Potato Head was the first ever toy to be advertised on TV. In 1985, he received four write-in votes in the election for Mayor of Boise, Idaho, USA.

In the year 2000, Jacob Dunnack forgot to bring his baseball when he brought his bat to his grandma's house. Needless to say, he was disappointed, but he came up with an ingenious way of making sure it didn't happen again. The JD Batball is a plastic baseball bat with a removable cap so the balls can be stored inside and won't get lost. This handy invention means kids can carry their bat and balls with one hand, while never worrying about forgetting or losing their baseballs again. Jacob Dunnack invented it when he was six years old.

To encourage use of his new invention, the shopping cart, market owner Sylvan Goldman hired fake shoppers to push the carts around his store in Oklahoma City, USA. He had to do this because the real customers didn't want to touch his invention.

Early Egyptian, Chinese, Greek and Roman writings describe numerous mixtures for toothpaste. The more palatable ingredients included powdered fruit, burnt shells, talc, honey and dried flowers. The less appetizing ones included mice and lizard livers.

The first commercial vacuum cleaner was so large it was mounted on a wagon. People threw parties in their homes so that guests could watch the new device do its job.

Becky Schroeder began her patenting career when she was just 14 years old. She put luminous paint on a piece of paper, and put it under her writing paper so that she could write in the dark. This invention has been used in all sorts of ways. Doctors use it in hospitals to read patients' charts at night without waking them, and astronauts use it when their electrical systems are turned down for recharging.

The first ballpoint pen was invented by Hungarian journalist Laslo Biro and his chemist brother, Georg, in 1938.

At just nine years old, in the 1850s, Margaret Knight began working in a cotton mill, where she saw a steel-tipped shuttle fly out of a loom and hit a nearby worker. As a result, Margaret devised her first invention: a shuttle restraining device. She went on to invent the machine that makes the square-bottomed paper bags still used for groceries in America.

Several people are credited with the invention of the flush toilet. Most famously, the hilariously named Thomas Crapper was the sanitary engineer who invented the valve-and-siphon arrangement that made the modern toilet possible. Another claimant to "the throne" was British inventor Alexander Cumming,

who patented a toilet in 1775. However, archeologists have discovered on the island of Crete the remains of what looks like a flush toilet that is believed to be 4,000 years old.

Galileo invented the thermometer in 1593.

Bullet-proof vests, fire escapes, windshield wipers and laser printers were all invented by women.

Robert Adler has the dubious distinction of being the father of the couch potato. Back in 1955, Adler was employed by what was then Zenith Radio Corporation, where he was asked to invent something that would allow viewers to turn down the TV volume without leaving their chairs. Early versions were attached to the set by a wire, which people could fall over. Then Adler hit on the idea of using sound waves, and the remote control was born.

As a health precaution, Alexander Graham Bell covered the windows in his home to block out what he thought were the harmful rays of the full moon!

The first rickshaw was invented in 1869 by an American Baptist minister, the Reverend E. Jonathan Scobie, to transport his invalid wife around the streets of Yokohama in Japan.

Melville Stone was a self-made man, who worked his way up from newspaper delivery boy to publisher of the *Chicago Daily News*. When Stone first started his newspaper in 1875, the price of a copy was one cent. Circulation rose rapidly at first, then levelled off. Then sales started to drop. When Stone investigated why fewer people were buying his paper, he discovered the problem had nothing to do with its quality, but largely that one-cent coins were in short supply, and nobody wanted to break a dollar for the sake of a one-cent newspaper. Stone decided he had to do something. First he visited the United States mint in Philadelphia and organised the shipment of barrels of one-cent coins to Chicago. His problem then became how to get the coins into circulation quickly. So Stone persuaded Chicago merchants to sponsor "odd-price sales", during which they would sell their merchandise for a cent under the regular price: $8.99, $10.99, $12.99 and so on. The odd prices did the trick. People had cent coins to get rid of again, and sales of the *Chicago Daily News* flourished once more.

In addition to the successful injection of the coins into the Chicago area, Stone had invented a phenomenon. The traders found that the penny off had a psychological effect on customers, making products seem cheaper ... and that's why so many prices today end in 99 (cents, for example).

FROM FOOT TO FERRARI

A Brief History of Driving

10,000 BC Nobody driving, anywhere.

6500 BC Wheel invented by Sumerians.

3500 BC Sumerians have animal-drawn vehicles.

500 BC First roads built by Persians.

1690 Early bicycle invented in France.

1765 Steam engine invented in the UK.

1824 Internal combustion engine first theorised by Sadi Carnot, France.

1868 First traffic signal, invented in the UK.

1884 Motorcycle invented in the UK.

1885 Car with internal combustion engine designed by Karl Benz, Germany.

1891 Front-engined car designed in France.

1908 Cars mass produced in the US.

1929 Ferrari founded, Enzo Ferrari, Italy.

FROM HUMBLE BEGINNINGS

Start Small - Get Big!

As a child, legendary physicist Albert Einstein was expelled from his school.

Chester Greenwood was born in Maine, USA, in 1858. A school dropout, he spent a lot of time ice skating, where his ears suffered from the cold. Making two loops from wire, he asked his grandmother to sew fur around them. Greenwood's Champion Ear Protectors were born and became famous. Chester made a substantial fortune supplying his Ear Protectors to, among others, the US Army. And in 1977, the state of Maine declared December 21 "Chester Greenwood Day!"

One morning in 1903, Albert J. Parkhouse arrived as usual at his workplace, the Timberlake Wire and Novelty Company in Michigan, USA, which specialised in making lampshade frames and other wire items. When he went to hang his hat and coat on the hooks provided for the workers, Parkhouse found they were all in use. Albert picked up a piece of wire, bent it into two large oblong hoops opposite each other, and twisted both ends at the centre into a hook. Then he hung up his coat and went to work.

The company apparently thought the "coat-hanger" was a good idea, because they took out a patent on it. In those days, companies were allowed to take out patents on any of their employees' inventions. The company made a fortune, and Albert never got a penny.

The discoverer of gravity, Isaac Newton, was thought to be a slow learner at school.

When Henry Ford started his production line car factory in the US, he was widely celebrated as a great innovator and copied throughout the world. His line wasn't such a hit with his workers, however. They complained that they were slaves to the machines and nine out of ten of the employees Ford hired walked out when they discovered their working conditions.

Nolan Bushnell spent more time running the games at a local amusement park than he did on his studies at the University of Utah, USA. In fact, he graduated at the bottom of his engineering class. His dreams of working for Disney's amusement empire were dashed – the company wouldn't hire him. Nolan day-dreamed about electronic versions of popular games. He invented Pong, the first video game, and went on to found the Atari video games company.

In 1850, the California gold rush was in full swing and everyday items were in short supply. Levi Strauss, a 20-year-old Bavarian immigrant, left New York for San Francisco with a small supply of rough canvas to sell for use as tents and wagon covers.
A prospector convinced Levi to make him some hardwearing work trousers from the canvas. They were a success, and other prospectors bought work trousers from Levi. Looking to improve on his design, Levi came across Serge de Nimes, a twill cloth from France that was hardy yet more comfortable to wear than his canvas. This cloth was to become known as "denim", and Levi's jeans were to become the most famous item of clothing on Earth. And they still are.

Orville Wright's first flight, which was largely responsible for the birth of the aviation industry, lasted a mere twelve seconds.

In 1886, Atlanta pharmacist John S. Pemberton invented a medicinal mixture for people who were tired, nervous or suffering from toothache. He took some of his new "health syrup" to a local shop. Instead of being mixed with ice water, as he had instructed, the syrup was mixed with soda water, making it fizzy. But Pemberton liked the taste and decide to market his health brew as a refreshing drink instead.

Pemberton's bookkeeper drew a fancy logo for the new product. The name they decided on was a mix of two of the ingredients, the coca leaf and the kola nut. It wasn't an immediate success – Mr Pemberton sold just fifty dollars' worth of "Coca-Cola" in his first year – but sales improved, and how! Today the world drinks one billion Coca-Cola Company products every single day.

Henry Ford, the man who brought cheap cars to the masses, also invented the barbecue-friendly charcoal briquette in 1920.

In 1933, Charles B. Darrow played a game he'd drawn on the cloth on his kitchen table – an exciting battle over property and fortune. He played at home with his family and friends, who found it addictive and asked for sets of their own. Charles went to work, making hand-made copies and selling them at four dollars each. Demand for the game grew beyond his ability to fill orders, and he took it to game company Parker Brothers, who rejected it. Undaunted, Charles continued to produce his hand-made editions and was highly successful. Finally Parker Brothers came to their senses and decided to buy the rights. The American people took to it in their millions. In 1935, under the Parker Brothers label, "Monopoly" became America's best-selling game. Darrow became a millionaire many times over, and today an estimated 500 million people worldwide play along.

Thomas Edison showed an inquisitive spirit at the tender age of six. He set the family barn on fire "just to see what it would do" and he tried to make a friend fly by feeding him a gas-producing laxative.

Earl Dickson's wife was rather accident prone, so he set out to develop a bandage that she could apply without help. He placed a small piece of gauze in the centre of a small piece of surgical tape, and what we know today as sticking plasters were born.

Joseph Priestly, the man who discovered oxygen, never took a science course.

In a vote for "Toy of the 20th Century", the winner was Lego. Game of the Century was Monopoly and Craze of the Century was the Yo-yo. Shortlisted entries included Action Man, Barbie, the teddy bear, Meccano, Scrabble, Mastermind and Trivial Pursuit.

Russian immigrant Conrad Hubert travelled to the US in 1890. He worked in a cigar store and a restaurant for a while, and he tried repairing watches. He was always broke. Conrad met a friend named Joshua Cowen who had invented a plant pot with a battery in it. Electricity from the battery made the flower in the pot light up when a button was pressed. Conrad decided he would try to sell these electric flower pots. Presently, Joshua became interested in something new and he sold his friend the flower pot idea for almost nothing. Conrad had an idea for a modification. He took the battery, the bulb and a paper tube and remade it into what he called "an electric hand torch." Hubert sold his invention as a novelty, but the usefulness of the torch soon became clear. When he died in 1928, Hubert was worth eight million dollars, which in 1928 was an awful lot of cash.

In 1907, James Murray Spangler, a janitor in Ohio, USA, deduced that the carpet sweeper he used was giving him a cough. He attached an old fan motor to his broom handle, using a pillow case as a dust collector. Spangler had invented an electric vacuum cleaner. He patented it in 1908, and formed the Electric Suction Sweeper Company. One of the first buyers was a cousin, whose husband, William H. Hoover, president of the Hoover Company, gave James a job. Before long there was a Hoover vacuum cleaner in homes everywhere.

In 1888, Marvin Stone made the first paper drinking straws. Before his straws, beverage drinkers used natural rye grass. Stone made his prototype straw by winding a strip of paper around a pencil and sticking it together. He decided the ideal straw was 22 centimetres (eight and a half inches) long with a diameter just narrow enough to stop a lemon pip.

CELEBRITY INVENTORS

More than One String to Their Bows

American War of Independence hero, Paul Revere, invented a process for cold rolling copper. The unpatented process was used to make plates for the boilers of early steamships.

Abraham Lincoln, congressman from Illinois, received a patent for "A Device for Buoying Vessels over Shoals". The idea of the invention was that if a ship ran aground in shallow waters, the bellows would be filled with air, and the ship would float clear. Lincoln became US President, and the model he whittled for his boat floater invention can be seen at the Smithsonian National Museum in Washington.

Edie Adams, singer and comedienne, patented a cigar holder-ring which she used in TV ads for Muriel cigars in the 1960s. It was designed to show women that it was ladylike to smoke cigars.

Danny Kaye, comedian and movie star, patented a "blow-out" party toy. Unlike the traditional "blow-out" toy that unfurls straight out, Kaye's unfurled in three directions at once.

American Statesman Benjamin Franklin invented bifocals because he hated having to wear two pairs of glasses.

Movie star Jamie Lee Curtis patented a nappy that ingeniously incorporates a handy pocket to hold moistened towelettes, so that the mucky baby and the means to clean it are always in the same place.

Rudyard Kipling, author of *The Jungle Book*, lived in Vermont, America in the 1890s. One chilly winter, he invented the game of snow golf. He painted his golf balls red so that they could be located in the white stuff.

A patent was issued in 1970 to movie legend Steve McQueen – a by-product of his racing cars hobby was the invention of a bucket seat.

Tom Sawyer author Mark Twain received a patent for "An Improvement in Adjustable and Detachable Straps for Garments". He later received two more patents: one for a self-pasting scrapbook and one for a game to help players remember important historical dates.

TV diver Jacques Cousteau co-invented the aqualung, allowing divers to stay in the depths of the sea for extended periods.

The first rubber balloons were made by English physicist and electrical pioneer, Michael Faraday, in 1824, for use in his experiments with hydrogen at the Royal Institution in London. Toy balloons were introduced by rubber maker Thomas Hancock the following year in the form of a kit consisting of a bottle of rubber solution and a syringe. Faraday went on to star on the £20 note for his scientific achievements, but didn't make a fortune from his balloons.

Hedy Lamarr, an Austrian movie actress, invented a radio guiding system for torpedoes which was used in World War Two. She gained the knowledge from her first husband, Fritz Mandl, a Viennese arms dealer who sided with the Nazis. Hedy drugged her maid to escape her husband and homeland, fled to America and became a Hollywood star.

Harry Houdini, the magician, received a patent for a "Diver's Suit" enabling the wearer to "quickly divest himself of the suit while being submerged and to safely escape and reach the surface of the water".

MR THUNDER & LIGHTNING

Nikola Tesla

Inventor and engineer Nikola Tesla was born in Croatia in 1856.

He first went to the US in 1884 to work for Thomas Edison, who had problems with his Direct Current system of electricity. He promised Tesla rich rewards if he could fix it. Tesla ended up saving Edison a fortune, but Edison went back on his agreement. Tesla resigned, and devised a better system for electrical transmission – the Alternating Current system we use in our homes today. He then invented the motors that are used in all household appliances. He was using fluorescent bulbs in his lab forty years before industry "invented" them.

At the World's Fair in 1893 in Chicago, he made glass tubes in the shapes of famous scientists' names – the first neon signs. He designed the world's first hydro-electric plant, located in Niagara Falls, and patented the first speedometer for cars.

The jealous Edison did his best to discredit Tesla at every turn, declaring that AC electricity was dangerous. So at the 1893 World Fair, Tesla demonstrated how safe AC was by passing it through his body to power light bulbs. He then shot lightning bolts to the crowd without harm. In 1898, he exhibited the first remote controlled model boat at Madison Square Garden, and he demonstrated the principles behind radio nearly ten years before Marconi. In 1943, the US Supreme Court ruled that Marconi's patents were invalid due to Tesla's previous work. Yet still he is not widely credited with the invention of radio.
But Tesla had his dark side too ...

He got a steam-driven oscillator to vibrate at the same frequency as the ground, creating an earthquake several miles in area. He stated that this technology could be used to split the Earth in half!

During World War One, the US government sought a way to detect German submarines, and put Edison in charge. Tesla proposed the use of energy waves – what we know today as radar – but Edison rejected Tesla's idea, and the world had to wait another 25 years for its invention.

Tesla died poor, aged 86, in 1943. In his lifetime, he received over 800 patents. Scientists continue to scour his notes, and many of his theories are just now being proven. Tesla might just be the greatest scientist who ever lived. If it wasn't for a jealous Thomas Edison, he would be a household name today.

If you enjoyed this book, you can find more amazing facts in the following books:

Title	ISBN
1000 of the World's Most Astonishing Facts	0 603 56067 9
The World's Most Amazing Animal Facts for Kids	0 603 56060 1
The World's Most Amazing Battle Facts for Kids	0 603 56098 9
The World's Most Amazing Crime Facts for Kids	0 603 56097 0
The World's Most Amazing Monster Facts for Kids	0 603 56104 7
The World's Most Amazing Planet Earth Facts for Kids	0 603 56062 8
The World's Most Amazing Science Facts for Kids	0 603 56062 8